salmonpoetry

Diverse Voices from Ireland and the World
Hex/PaulBregazzi

Hare's Breath

Brian Kirk

Published in 2023 by
Salmon Poetry
Cliffs of Moher, County Clare, Ireland
Website: www.salmonpoetry.com
Email: info@salmonpoetry.com

Copyright © Brian Kirk, 2023

ISBN 978-1-915022-46-2

All rights reserved. No part of this publication may be reproduced or transmitted in any form or by any means, electronic or mechanical, including photography, recording, or any information storage or retrieval system, without permission in writing from the publisher. The book is sold subject to the condition that it shall not, by way of trade or otherwise, be lent, resold or otherwise circulated without the publisher's prior consent in any form of binding or cover other than that in which it is published and without a similar condition, including this condition, being imposed on the subsequent purchaser.

Cover Image: *'Irish Hare' by Rosaleen Fleming*
Cover Design & Typesetting: *Siobhán Hutson Jeanotte*

Printed in Ireland by Sprint Print

Salmon Poetry gratefully acknowledges the support of
The Arts Council / An Chomhairle Ealaíon

for Martha & Ciarán & the future

Contents

Hare's Breath	9
Palimpsest	10
Cuckoo	11
Kingdom	12
Windfall	13
Belturbet Under Frost	14
Googling My Parents	15
Hard Swallows	16
In The Pit	17
That Last Summer	18
My First Infatuation	19
Sour	20
Sundays in June	21
Hydra	22
Bully	23
How You Lived Then	24
There will be time…	25
Present Tense	26
A Purpose	27
Exile	28
Excursion into Philosophy	29
Knockout	30
Hibakusha	31
The Last Days of Pompeii	32

Train Dreams	34
Fire & Flood	35
Houses	36
Seaside Fools	37
Gaia	38
Hawk	39
Letting Go	40
Staying Home	41
Dog Days	42
Christmas Work	44
Deepfake	45
Mutatis Mutandis	46
Sun	47
Ahimsa	48
The Workshop	49
Out of Time	50
The Book of the Dead	51
Busker	52
Multiverse	53
Small Things	54
Despatches	56
The Invisible House	58
Acknowledgements	61
About the author	62

Hare's Breath

I came here to work
but needed to stop.
That first day, tramping
up Bolus Head, mentally
pulling together the threads
of an unwritten story,
trapped between ocean
and mountain, eyes bent
to the road, sheep droppings
bunched like black grapes.
I walked as words withered,
eyes scanning the cliffs
and those sheep, improbably
balanced on a craggy incline.
Hooded crows fought the wind.
Then I saw her, shapeshifter,
iambic, limber, crossing the hill.
Frozen, lungs filled with wind –
a hare's breath – I held it
a moment before it escaped.

Palimpsest

Kids almost grown but the house more crowded than ever.
I'm clearing out the room downstairs, full of accumulated
junk, half-forgotten remnants of a life, tokens, totems
of another person's past. I come across all these pages,
some typed, some handwritten, that I can't remember
writing and among them I find the stories you wrote,
typed on the sad Underwood with the sticky ribbon,
and on the back of one a poem I wrote, about you sleeping,
when we knew or cared nothing about futures, in the flat
in Canning Town after a night of drinking in The Scud.

Cuckoo

I saw some pictures in a book;
a bird in flight, tail feathers splayed,
a hulking chick, jaws open wide,
being fed by a tiny robin.

Still April evenings when the world
was young, I heard a limpid song
carry across the fields and hang
in twilight air, suspending time.

Two notes, a pause, repeat once more.
I yearned to see the bird that called
from far away; it seemed to meld
the fear I nurtured with a helpless

hope that childhood couldn't name.
I set out as the day declined
and found my bird – it was ordained –
sublime, enthroned on a fencepost.

I took a stone up off the ground
and aimed it at the regal bird –
I craved the thing and not the word.
My hands shook as it flew away.

Kingdom

My father cut the hedges, planted beds, stored fuel up for the winter months,
built fires in chilly waiting rooms. He didn't say a lot, but when he spoke
you listened if you knew what was good for you. We arrived one by one, full

of promise, poor but well turned out, fed but always hungry for a taste
of something more. We didn't lick it off the ground. Despite the well-kept
borders of his world, he indulged a dream of other ways of living and daily

bought a ticket to a life on the far side of respectability. Horses and the football
pools promised a way of getting by, but winning only came in small amounts
at lengthy intervals, so he put his shoulder to the wheel, gave up the drink,

cut back the fags, was frugal in every way, worked every day so that his children
had the chance he was denied, determined that his life would have some meaning
by creating opportunities for us. He became an archetype of sorts, a poster boy

for Church and State united, a man only De Valera could have dreamed.
But we grew up and let him down. We craved different things, our childhoods spent
gazing out beyond the hedges that he trimmed, dreaming another kind of life

outside the fortress that he built from duty, faith, and love. The foundations
were unstable, the things he thought would last forever soon would crack: work
and order couldn't bear the weight. His kingdom didn't last. No kingdom does.

Windfall

It looked so easy on the face of it.
Pick eight home wins, four draws
or four aways (these would pay out less).
He always went for eight score draws
chosen from the four divisions,
the Treble Chance: a maximum
of twenty-four points to be scored.
Week in week out he made his exes
on the coupon, paid his cash –
why wouldn't he when Cyril Grimes
from Hampshire won half a million
only weeks before?
Good money after bad, that's what
we thought, but every Saturday
the teleprinter hypnotised us
as we watched in hope until
the classified results announced
our disappointment with
a falling cadence.

Belturbet Under Frost

for my parents, Terry & Anne

I marvel at the flawlessness of things,
his shiny shoes, kind words, the cap he tossed
in her direction, and the songs he sings
that take him back. Belturbet under frost
those winter mornings when he'd leave his digs,
visit her shop before the Belfast train –
the street in darkness still – to purchase fags,
but really to see her. He can't refrain
from idling in the warmth of her shy smile
while the gruff owner indicates the time:
'Shouldn't you be on your way this while?'
He lingers by the door as the sun climbs
over Kilconny Bridge and rushing Erne.
The stations pass; she waits for his return.

Googling My Parents

When I Googled my parents there were no matching results, only
traces of others who bore the same names, living counterfeit lives

that failed to reflect the authenticity of monochrome days I recall
in that house by the railway line, where the sun shone all summer,

where huge ash trees waved their hysterical arms in March winds,
and a thin frost painted a dull world silver on the shortest days.

My parents don't exist in the world, real or virtual, but are trapped
in stacks of wrinkled snaps; they look out at me with unseeing eyes,

perplexed, uncertain, frozen in a moment snatched from time. I know
there's no option to reboot, no going back except through memory's

patched-up matinee. From time to time, to kick-start reminiscence,
I read their names in stone among a host of other names on stones

ranged on a blanket of land that rolls down to the sea near home.
Perhaps the mind is a hard drive scanning the residue of lives

no longer with us, its circuits switching on and off, firing in dreams
where the dead arise, their voices talking out of the bright cloud.

Hard Swallows

Every summer they came back, hard swallows
with pinched city faces, bullet heads, black boots
and braces, ink tattoos and traces of abuse
we took for attitude. Sitting on the wall
across from Leisureland, drinking cider,
spitting, shirts off in the midday sun.
We crossed the road to pass them,
trying to look down but our eyes
were drawn to these exotic summer
visitors, thirsty for a sip of urban
squalor, bored with the blunt routine
of school and farm in this backwater.
By evening their numbers grew,
the squad car took a turn around
the town, the air felt heavy like a storm
might break. The pubs won't serve
but the dark dunes welcome them
along with certain local girls who can't resist
their tattooed arms, flat vowels that bend
their names into a novel sound, unfamiliar,
overwhelmed with wistful possibility,
until the word gets out and there's murder
on the street. While happy families sleep
it starts with threats, builds to shouts and screams,
breaking glass, car engines roaring down
the darkened street. Sun rises and the town
is not the same, shopkeepers boarding
broken windows, sweeping glass out of the road,
boiling kettles to remove the blood that dries
like clotted paint on concrete. Every summer
was the same, every summer they came back.

In The Pit

So many excuses could be given
for my almost fatal carelessness:
the innocence and ignorance of youth,
the negligence of adults, the hidden
dangers of the farmyard. I thought my life
was over. After a short struggle, I realised
that I was only hastening my end, but still
my arms and legs reached out to find
a base that wasn't there. How deep the shit
was, I'll never know. Time slowed yet didn't stop,
allowed me to relive my life, see the faces
of the ones I loved, feel a child's sorrow
for the ending of a story that had only just begun.
I called and called but no one heard;
I wondered was I silent, struck dumb
as the broken implements in my field
of vision: the rusted harrow and the buckled
wheel, the busted trailer sunk in mud.
Just as I began to drown in that foul sea
the farmer threw a rope, instructed me
to tie it round myself. He pulled me like
a young weed from concrete, rootless –
dying all this time since I was saved.

That Last Summer

That June I left national school behind –
long trousers, blazers beckoned,
but I found myself in shorts and sandals.
Sun baked the earth until it cracked;
water was cut off for hours or pressure
low. Plants died in the garden while
the last summer of freedom – before work
in fields or glasshouses – spilled out
around my feet. Those final weeks when
I was still a child, lost for hours under
a high sun, blue sky; before adults
insisted I toughen up, not be so sensitive,
show a bit of gumption and not be
always moping and alone when
every other child my age was doing
stuff, learning new things, trying
to place one foot inside the future.
Inside, they huddled round the set,
agog to see Tomorrow's World,
but I remember the sun setting over
an August stubble field, my world
ablaze, not wanting night to fall.

My First Infatuation

Her uncle drove a red sports car with the top down,
wind plucking stray locks from his combover. The engine idled
as I watched, crouched over my old bike with the leaky
valve. She was his favourite, but my sixteen-year-old self read
something more in it; the copy of *Lolita* that I thumbed but never
borrowed from the library. Imagination flamed: the older man,
the younger girl, a gash of lipstick on her smiling mouth,
his gloved hand brushing against bare thigh as he went down
a gear at the bottom of Ballustree. Her wild hair dancing
in the wind; a tightness in my chest, them sitting two abreast,
smiling, growling engine spitting smoke, tyres dusting me
with sand blown in from the strand onto Main Street. I wheeled
my bike back home but couldn't find the wherewithal
to catalogue the squalid contents of my teenage mind.

Sour

She came in the summer on an airless day
when time dragged and flies beat themselves
senseless against the pane. Bored, you let
yourself be snagged by her red hair and lips; the rumour
of excitement in a dreary seaside town was just enough
to push you into action. Her saliva on an apple
that you shared drove you to distraction. July heat
made you feel weak and other things you wouldn't
care to mention to your mother, but it was fine,
the face she showed to others was angelic, pure.
Lonely, miserable, I didn't stand a chance against
the two of you. I wanted to be liked, that's all,
but you were after something more. She knew it,
let you have a taste. It made my stomach turn.

Sundays in June

When summer Sundays leaned into evening,
the sky was clear, the light began to dim a little
and a tired silence occupied the best chairs
in the house leaving you uncomfortable, distracted.
If only night would fall, if only day would end,
you might stay home. The TV was no help so you went
out into the back yard where nature pretended to exist.
The cars on the main road called out to you, sending
you back to your room where you counted out the few
remaining notes. The bus would be passing in half an hour.
In the town, the amusement arcade would be hammering
the senses, pubs would be filling up, drinkers spilling
out onto the sandy street, red faces soaking up pints
and the last rays of the sun as if nothing else mattered.

Hydra

In July you embraced reincarnation;
under a hot sun lizards became lighter
and soul shone through the surface of our skins.
The wheel of life turned summer to autumn,
winter into spring; there was a pattern,
a cycle to everything. Now all the sun-cream
in the world can't re-hydrate the wizened
epidermis of those days; scales flake,
ride on the surface of pure light
reflecting falling night in liver spots.
We learned at last how flesh capitulates
in time – cold comfort that the soul persists,
sequestered in feigned heaven or false hell.
Better to quit on time than be a Hercules,
lopping the heads off monsters to the end.

Bully

I think about the boy who bullied me,
I wonder did we pre-ordain his life,
consign him to the Joy, a nobody.
Perhaps he settled down and found a wife,
forgave the teachers and the priests who beat
him so that he might be a better man
and not a guttersnipe ghosting Main Street
day and night. Time ran on, there was no plan,
no guarantee of comfort or success.
They lied to us just as they lied to him,
but he was bolder, ready to transgress
while we were timid souls, pale synonyms
for cowardice. With rules we broke his will,
with formal words in verse I cage him still.

How You Lived Then

And were you really seeking after truth?
Certainly, cerebral books were read,
but youth they say is wasted on the youth;
most of the time you lived inside your head.
That your life would prove no better than the rest –
lacking ambition, stunted and depressed –
was your great fear when you were starting out.
You watched commuters hurrying from rooms,
bodies imbued with energy, minds with doubt,
racing to offices, hospitals and tombs.
A young man's fancy runs to the extreme
sustaining ennui's obstinate regime.

There will be time...
i.m. Gerry Flanagan

I was angry with you.
I was hurt,
the way you left with no goodbye.
For years I've been waiting
for a note of explanation to turn up.
Winters, summers came and went,
the usual blather about dying and rebirth.
How could I know the happiness I'd see,
the hours of thoughtless play, the journeys
I would make, the joyful homecomings?
Long days spent on my own, content
or agitated, the meals I shared with loved ones,
the crops I harvested, the fruit I left to rot.

Present Tense

The time is now. In order to stay sane we're told
to live in the moment, as if that's a good place.

The past is another country, its borders closed
to those who choose to embrace the still instant

before it turns over and settles back into itself.
The future is nothing but a lack of imagination,

a view you'll never see. Consider the bird, the tree,
the flowers on your walk; they die each time

you turn away and rise again the moment you return.
Now is the time to choose. Inhale. Take each day as a gift,

a present from a sleeping world that never dreams.

A Purpose

Sleep leaves you wrung out in the early morning,
snaking down unfamiliar paths, restless,
uncertain if day is here yet. Birds cry outside,
some call it singing, but you're not convinced.
Low sun in the east or the west hardly matters,
your eyes hurt either way. Breath comes short
and quick, heart pumping blood through veins.
Initiate the ritual, open your eyes, don't fear the quotidian,
welcome the unknown. Shake off those dreams,
they're no longer real, cancel your appointments
even though the only thing that's certain
is you have nowhere else to be right now.

Exile

All the rented rooms you lived in down the years.
The damp-stained walls, the smelly carpets,
sticky floors, unsteady tables, unstuffed chairs;
the furtive places you returned to at the end
of busy or aimless days. This was meant to be
your life, but it was passing by – and you
were letting it – unable or unwilling to graft
meaning onto habit. Remember that first year
when you moved away? The fear you felt,
the growing panic that you were floating free,
but not in a pleasant way. The bed became a raft,
bobbing on a swelling tide on those nights
when you drank too much, the soap-sour
taste uprising in your throat. Those days
you only thought about returning;
day and night you dreamed of going home,
but you wouldn't let yourself be tempted.
It was a kind of purging, a way to make
your life seem real. Just one more week,
a month, a year – you steeled your will.
How could you know that it would disappear?

Excursion into Philosophy
Edward Hopper, 1959

We are only ever alone.

Sharing a sunlit room, our backs almost touching
could be miles apart.

The discarded book remains open,
read or unread;
the moment unfolds,

trapped between two rectangles of light.

Outside the sky is sky blue, the ground in shadow.
Inside it's awful.

Something is over, something new
has yet to be born. Knowledge comes
with the heft of a blow.

Light opens out as space closes in.

Are beginnings and endings the same?

Knockout

Have a drink to hamper memory,
take a pill to quell the tremor;
stay at home and hide from others
whose fathers, mothers might
remember what you said or did
that time you lost it years ago.
The silence is an empty bucket
you must fill with stuff inside
your head – spill it out onto
the road and keep on spilling.
Don't ask questions you already
know the answers to. If you must
go out, then wear a belted coat and hat,
a private eye abroad in daylight taking notes
you later will destroy – there's no good
keeping things, public things
or private things. Alone in crowds,
in crowds alone, you fear, despise
in equal measure: and that is fair.
Fair too your gaunt reflection
in shop windows, a ghost
self-haunting in the day and night.
If pressed stick always to the facts,
names and dates that can be proven;
the where, the when and how
are questions you no longer
may allow. Smile if you can, wince
if you must. The blow will come, so
call it by its name, evince indifference,
accept the fated final ferocity
before you hug the floor.

Hibakusha*

Somehow after a fire the forest
starts again, first with weeds
and grasses followed by scrub trees.
After a time the animals come back.
In Bikini Atoll crabs and coral thrive
where people do not live. In Chernobyl,
against all odds, nature flourishes
in poisoned silence free of man.
In Ukraine, families flee in the face of war,
gather up what they can carry and begin
again, because what else is there to do?
In Hiroshima and Nagasaki, after the blasts,
black shadows appeared on the buildings
and the streets. Wind and rain erased
them over time except for those preserved
in the Peace Memorial Museum, while
on the streets the living carried on.

* Hibakusha are survivors of the 1945 atomic bombing of Hiroshima and Nagasaki

The Last Days of Pompeii

You have the right to remain silent
but you should really speak.
The barbarians are at the gate
and plague is rife among the soldiery.
Remember, anything you say may be
used against you in a court of law,
but who cares? There may not be
a court anon. Titus will be dead within the year,
a victim of his brother's ambition.
You could go to Pompeii, kill some time
in the brothels there, rely on Pliny's ships
to save you when Vesuvius erupts.
But Terra Mater will always find you,
take you when you least expect it.
You've ignored her for too long,
shrugged off the views of sages,
laughed at those who demonstrate
their worries for the future of the empire.
You have, of course, the right to have
an attorney present before and during
questioning and, if you can't afford that,
to have one appointed without cost to you,
to represent you before and during questioning.
By then it will be far too late.
Domitian will be laying down the law,
upsetting the elders in the Senate; disease
will bed in for the long winter ahead.
You have the freedom to die quietly,
infecting others as you go. And when you die
we'll bury you gratis in a convenient mass grave.

Religion? Don't make me laugh –
we are as flies to wanton boys etc...
They promised you the rising tide,
and it will come like a tsunami
across the bay of Naples; the trickle down
has been delayed, but it can be procured
at a price no one can afford.

Train Dreams

When Denis Johnson died I went to my local library –
built with money donated by the philanthropist Carnegie –
borrowed a copy of *Train Dreams* and read it in his memory.
All week I'd been reading his stories on my phone on the tram;
gems buried in the archives of the New Yorker and the Paris Review.
They explode in your mind when you read them, infect your thoughts
and spread like a disease to the imagination. The future offers
itself in a peculiar light at a precarious slant, the past disturbed
re-settles in a surprising form. Your memories get re-written, borrowed,
read, returned, stranger but truer than they'd been before.

Fire & Flood

I read about the fires across the Amazon and thought of the rain we'd had this summer. **After a long time** even **Noah saw the sun** but we weren't yet **emerging through the grey. Although the rain** was finally dying off in places, it **still fell in squalls.** I wondered about the creatures abroad in it, those pairs that Noah saved – **the animals undone, confined and restless in their stalls** – would they have rather taken their chances in the flood? Appalled perhaps – **the plain a distant memory,** they **bawled their pain across the waters that unfolded to the end of vision's range**. I wondered how much rain it would take to quench those forest fires. I thought of the dying animals and how **after the raven's loss, a dove was sent to try to find dry land.** It must have seemed a hopeless enterprise, a vain attempt, until **returning at the last with olive leaf** that symbolic bird spoke in the only way it could, a message **that told of God's assurances to spare the few who chose the path of just belief.** We never pause to think about the fate of all the rest; we stick with the story of those **who built a boat when others would despair**, a mad-cap notion to preserve each species, **a haven for all creatures from God's wrath**, but not all creatures – one forlorn conscriptee from each sex, incarcerated on a stinking boat **until**, despairing, halfway mad, **rejoicing, they found Ararat.**

Houses

Years ago, my older brother told me, by the time
you finish school these fields will be gone,
buried under houses as far as the eye can see.

The hedges will be swept away, roads widened
to let traffic flow with ease, although there will
be no jobs left to do, no places left to go.

He didn't say that birds would fly and not return,
or how dying foxes would eat the spills from bins
at back doors; how flowers would fail, choked by nettles

and yellow grass that scratches the edge of concrete,
tarmacadam, steel. Did he dream that trees would stoop
like old people waiting in line with outstretched arms,

or that the wind would blow, hot then cold, broadcasting
the drone of huge machines excavating groundworks
for houses, houses as far as the eye can see?

Seaside Fools

We are fools who live beside the sea,
we do not know the names of birds
who feed along the water's edge.
The fish that live beneath the waves are strange
to us, the vegetation too; for us it's all seaweed,
a smelly nuisance strewn across the hard sand
where we walk our dogs each day under pewter
skies, the island in the distance, sometimes nearer,
sometimes far away, depending on conditions
which we take no notice of unless to bring a rain-proof
coat or hat and scarf. We are seaside dwellers,
fools to ours and future generations, we cannot
tell if the tide is coming in or going out.

Gaia

Five times the tide rose on the broken land
and as it did the moon sipped on the sea,
bloated, weary, an August bumble bee
drunk on the last of summer's contraband.
And we, marooned inside our sanctuary,
having withdrawn from the world and a life
that drained us, turn over a new leaf
in the silence of a closed library,
reading the future from an open book,
while outside the present happens heedless
of what we think, our hopes or foolish dreams.
We're dust, and nature doesn't give a fuck
about our self-importance or regrets:
one day our books will float away in streams.

Hawk

All summer you grumbled how magpies woke you in the mornings
with their screeching and the scratching of their feet on the roof

above our open bedroom window. I was always grateful for
the splendour of their perfect pied apparel as they hopped across

the garden grass. One day, when they ganged up on the cat
and sent her running, I changed my mind. I never bought

the old wives' tales of bad luck they might bring, worried
only for the smaller birds who no longer came to feed.

You blamed them, of course, and I began to think you might be right.
Then, this morning at the bin I saw a clutch of feathers on the grass;

I noticed how the cat was drawn to it as soon as she stepped out.
I knew exactly what it was, marvelling how the black had dulled

to ash, a pale facsimile of what it was in life. Turning towards
the door I saw, some feet away, the wings outspread – angelic –

the innards eaten out; the hollow breast revealed a blood-red
heart of flesh. What did this dreadful thing? And then I saw

among the longer blades of grass, the perfect severed head,
plague doctor mask with shiny pate, the eyes like ebony.

Letting Go

In May you threw good money after bad:
food, shoes, a magic pen that wipes out stains.
Too long at home, uncertain, somewhat sad,
watched days drift by through dusty window panes.
Distracted for a while by phone, iPad –
how like a battery concentration drains.
A new way has arrived and you endure
with little choice, distracted and unsure.

The summer passed and nothing seemed to change.
You formed a bond with absence, now distance
became the calculus of safety's range.
Stumbling on the path of least resistance,
when you moved at all, denying how strange
the world had grown, proceeding in a trance,
no longer able to remember when
you dreamed you had your old life back again.

September came, October following,
you opened up your eyes as from a sleep
and saw the dancing trees were fallowing;
oak, blackthorn, ash, elm, juniper and beech,
red, gold and bronze, the green leaf yellowing
to white. You understood such beauty cannot keep;
the trees, despite their agitation, also know
these colours are a sign they must let go.

Staying Home

Churches vacant, the public houses closed,
families forced to make some conversation.
Monday morning, not a sinner on the road

to work or school; empty buses brake, unload
dead air that might be carrying contagion.
Churches vacant, the public houses closed,

you hide in plain sight in your own abode.
Remove your homely self to your workstation;
it's Monday morning, not a sinner on the road

and that report you promised won't upload.
You calculate per cent of population.
Churches vacant, the public houses closed,

the things you knew for certain now unknown,
faith to doubt to boredom, concatenation.
Monday again, not a sinner on the road –

why would there be? – the speed of life has slowed
to a limp, a dying generation:
churches vacant, the public houses closed,
Monday morning, not a sinner on the road.

Dog Days

Summer came scampering into the house
this year, uncalled for, dragging garden
smells on muddy paws and a new silence
coloured by a yellow, ever-present sun
that threatened but never delivered storms.
On humid nights you were visited in dreams

by memories of failure, the unfulfilled dreams
of your youth. You cowered while the house
held its breath in expectation of a storm
that never came. Something stirred in the garden;
Orion's dog slept under a shade in the sun,
tongue lolling, his breath breaking the silence,

laboured, hoarse, excavating the silence
of your mind, making room for more dreams,
vague anxieties fostered under a glaring sun.
You grew accustomed to being prisoner in your house,
the known world extended to the bottom of the garden,
no further, but the TV brought you closer to the *sturm*

und drang of peoples tearing each other apart. Storms
in teacups to you who measured out each day in silence.
Heat spilled out the open windows into the garden,
searing the grass, choking flowers while you dozed, dreaming
of disease, death and decay consuming the house.
Outside it was worse, speared under a burning sun,

unable to pretend that everything was normal, to sun
yourself and watch the skies, wait for the storm
to pass. Your impatience could not be housed
by an absence that knew no other form but silence.
Worse than sleeping was the waking dream,
finding yourself alone and standing in the garden,

looking around, naming what you see: garden,
grass, trees, bent flowers dying under the hot sun,
knowing you haven't been away, just in a dream,
wishing to hell that something would change, the storm
might break, the children next door might assault the silence.
After a while you give up, go back inside the house.

After this summer of silences, you are primed to storm
the garden's barricades and reach up to pull the sun
down out of the sky, into your fever dreams, your hollow house.

Christmas Work

The kind of work that only you could do,
that's what you do. What choice have you?
Hours of waiting around that might seem
pointless to the passer-by, but mean
everything to those who understand the cost
of land and property. In winter, when the days
grow short, when villages turn in on themselves,
you remain like a scarecrow after harvest,
for there is still work to be done, a principle
at stake to be maintained. You stand
as a warning to the displaced and the weary
to keep out and stay out; and as a threat
to the righteous to mind their business,
to keep on driving past the empty house,
the barren fields; ignore the shadowed men,
the dogs, the unmarked vans, and keep their eyes
on the road ahead, the winking lights of home.

Deepfake

I'm happy to mind my own business,
to turn a blind eye, so long as I'm left alone.
When people complain, I can't help but think:
boo hoo, you have only yourself to blame. In art
I look for beauty and truth, admire the pathos
of suffering, a violence of style, the tragedy
of a prophesied Dystopia. But I won't relent
because there is a line between life and poetry
that must never ever be crossed – until it is.
Then it's too late, and I am the story; lies spew
from smiling mouths that no one could believe,
so I turn to my friends seeking solidarity, denouncing
fake news and myth. Meantime, behind headlines
runs a dumb show of death, forests burning, cities
in flood, and there's my face, superimposed on the rapist's.

Mutatis Mutandis

When Heraclitus talked about the river
never being the same, he was half right.
And when he talked about the person
never being the same, he was half right too.
The old curmudgeon knew the only constant
is change and only change can endure.
The river knows this too without being told,
has always known it in the way of all rivers,
in spate and trickle, pool and flow.
Our natures have become unnatural,
and all the learning in the world
can't teach us what the swallow knows
or what compels the salmon to struggle
against the current, never doubting.
We must re-learn the lesson every day,
we're not the same as we were yesterday:
I'm not the same, you're not the same,
he's not the same, she's not the same,
we're not the same, ye're not the same. No.
You are not the same. They are not the same.

Sun

Even as the weather goes to hell
we glory in the memory of heat.
Days when we left the house without a coat,
ignored whatever the world might have to sell,
boarded a bus and found ourselves in town
among the crowds, as if we had just stepped
out for a paper. These selfish moments shine,
reflect a careless time when no one or thing
could move us to be other than we were,
like rude Diogenes basking in the sun.

Ahimsa

The real world is unknown,
the known unreal, I tell myself.
We argue on the sea front
amid the day-trippers
and down-and-outs.
I want to walk away
but follow you instead.
At the aquarium
everything flip-flops.
The squid withdraw
while the ray over-act,
flapping and splashing
as they move in a circle.
Outside there will
be ice-cream, shouts
of animal joy
and reprimands,
but in this sanctum
there is peace.
I follow you down
to the shark tank
where it's even darker;
there are no words,
only the whispered awe
of children soaked
in the shadows
of silent fathers.
I tell myself,
Ahimsa is the highest virtue.
I find you at the coffee stand,
red-eyed, and beg forgiveness.

The Workshop

I put my trauma on a page,
brought it to the old school hall
and showed it to the group.
Reassured by their insouciance –
I could tell they'd heard it all before –
in awe of jaded urbane slouch,
wry raised eyebrow, cool remark.
When my turn came to speak
I kept it brief; I praised where I felt
praise was earned, stayed silent
on the parts I thought were weak.
That's just my nature, always trying
to appease. But other minds can be unlike
my own. They took my words and stacked
them in a pile that showed them small,
or isolated them so they looked puny
on the page. One said: *the poem turns here,
it quickens on this word that cannot take
the strain.* Another said: *this phrase is death,
it pulls me from the poem, undoes what little good
was done up to that stage.* I thought about
my hurt while others spoke. I wondered
why I'd brought it here where no one knows
my life beyond an abstruse story on a sheet
of paper. Why did I come here? To make it better
or more real? I left before the others could invite
me for a drink. I worked on it some more
when I got home. It only made things worse.

Out of Time

with apologies to Amergin

I am past, present and future
I am equally absent in each
I am Columbus, all at sea but refusing to ask for directions
I am Thomas, seeing the wounds but still not convinced
I am the sly grin that says there's no smoke without fire
I am a crowd baying for Barabbas' release
I am uncomfortable in my own skin
I am a heart clogged with trans fats
I am a head for forgetting
I am an insult imagined
I am revenge plotted on sleepless nights but never carried out
I am a spreader of scandal
A repeater of banalities
I expect every road to rise with me
Embarrassment is my constant companion
Shame is the uncle I keep locked away in the asylum
I am Joe Bergin lost on the back roads of Laois blaming his wife
I am the hollow laugh, the sour puss
The one who can be relied on to say nothing
I am the hand on the tiller as we head towards the rocks
Who knows the locations of the graves of his ancestors?
Who will not admit the impermanence of things?
Who will stand by and watch the sun set on the world?

The Book of the Dead

A shadow at the back door mimes a cry, a magpie watches from the wall.
The year is dying but the weather is still warm enough. You let her in
and feed her while your own meal cooks. She must take precedence.

When you finally sit down, she is asleep, a breathing bracket placed
around some books on the good sofa. She shouldn't be there, but you let
her stay because you know it won't be long before she goes. Last night

she sat upon your lap and dozed – oh how unlike her! She understands
that time is short. You wonder does she rue the times she shunned
you when you needed love, feel guilty about those nights she stayed

out late. You stood at the back door, frozen, calling out her name
to no avail. You often sensed that she was there, outside the reach
of light that leaked from the open door, but you can't be sure.

You get up later, so much later, and she's back, complaining
that you locked her out all night. The goddess disregards remorse,
but later she absolves you, brings you gifts: a field mouse, pygmy shrew

or a luckless sparrow who, unlike Icarus, flew too near the ground.
Her hunting days are over now. She leaves her food to fester
on the dish and walks away, complaining. You think you understand

these sounds but they are cryptic, aural hieroglyphs, that signify one thing
only, that time is running out. The next day brings indignities unworthy
of a deity: the carry box, the room that stinks of piss and disinfectant,

the gloved hands of the vet that quell her spirit. The omens aren't good.
There is no other way. You stroke her head and beg for her forgiveness…

Busker

While he played
we stood around
exchanging smiles
though no one spoke.
And when he stopped
some clapped or dropped
a coin into his hat
while others looked away.
Some turned their backs
on him, distracted
by their private cares,
but we gathered
the residue of melody
and pulled it around us
like an old coat
buttoned up against
a new chill in the air.

Multiverse

"Every kairos is a chronos, but not every chronos is a kairos."
Hippocrates

Once upon a time in a land not very far away
I was a version of myself before I met a prototype of you;
two opposites collided in imagined space, auguring
a future harmony, unexpected but awaited.
We sensed an opportunity, a spontaneous knitting
of perspectives, gauche, sophisticated beyond the accidents
of birth. We shared a sense of quest fated in a sacred logos,
set forth upon an epic journey that took us back

to here, where we are now. The sense of so much living
crammed into moments that collapse, unfold in arcane
sequences, altered as occasion might demand. Dates
like fairy lights strung across a darkening garden when the party's
almost over and the next day hovers in the branches; dim outline
of morning promising fatigue and argument, desire asleep
in bed beside you long after the alarm's been silenced
by a hand much like the one that knocks, demands you meet

the future; a concept that will be elusive yet concrete, indefinite,
but growing sharper every day. It's time to rise and rush into
that future, past the present, outrunning time's arrow, outpacing
yourself in the narrow stream of things that constitute a life. Keep going,
you must be ready always for the moment when the stars align,
before the arrow falls or after memory unspools, a remnant on the floor.
Light dies, and when a different light emerges, more blinding than before,
you believe in magic once again; a child cries, an old man dries his eyes.

Small Things

for Catherine Corless

She wraps a stone in an old sweet paper, just like she's seen
the older girls do, offers it to a streel of a thing from the home,
watching big eyes light up for a moment before going out.

The girl was famished; what if she'd put it in her mouth?
Some say a stone sucked from time to time, will trick
the stomach into thinking it's being fed, releasing enzymes

to work on what's not there, adding a peculiar ache
to habitual hunger pangs. She often thinks of it, that meanness,
a small thing that stays with her, won't let her be. Just leave it alone,

that's what some people said, why go upsetting the holy nuns?
Even after she counted them out, painstakingly adding new names
to the list of dead babies, the causes of death: measles, TB,

hunger, pneumonia, neglect. Four euro for a certificate,
paid out of her own pocket, the only proof they once lived.
All gone. Small lives that nobody noticed or cared about,

little deaths that deserved no more than the stroke of a pen.
Not the word of a priest, a sad song from a choir, a slow walk
to a grave where earth falling on oak could be the final, solemn

sound before the tears of loved ones filled the air and soft words
telling the story of little him or her and what they liked or hated, or how
they smiled when the gardener's dog chased pigeons from the seeded

rows in Spring, or how the tiny fingers curled about the handle of a spoon at supper time, or how their shiny cheeks went dipping in cold water at Halloween, russet as the apples in the bowl. Small things I know.

She found their names and gave them back to us although we weren't sure, surprised to find we needed them as much as they had needed us back then. Each one so small, a tiny gift, a question asked and answered with her love.

Despatches

*i.m. Edward Sheridan, Petty Officer Telegraphist,
Royal Navy (1917 – 1945)*

Struck amidships,
the gaping hole invited water
and the final memories

of a short life lived
in search of *Boys' Own* exploits.
You watched the ranks

of swallows on the wires,
when shadows lengthened
on a midlands farm,

and dreamt of Java,
Alexandria, Ceylon. First
time you ran away,

they sent you back:
too young. But two years later
they took you as a Boy

at fifteen years, six months.
You learned your trade in peacetime,
long before the Munich Crisis

sparked orders to weigh
anchor and embark for Freetown
and a protracted war;

tapping the code
that sent the words
to safety beyond the boom

of wave and ocean
spume to harbours
that were havens

where all futures met.
But yours was not assured.
Although you dodged the fate

of *Perseus*, it took a winter
visitor to sink the *Lapwing*
in the Barents Sea.

Homing torpedo from a U-boat
broke the boat in two.
A wife and daughter

waited, hoped a message
would not come. The worst
arrived in Royal livery,

O.H.M.S. and postage paid.
By order of the King
and the First Lord

of the Admiralty:
*he gave his life to save
mankind from tyranny.*

The Invisible House

In dreams I take the train from town, shunting through grass
embankments to the station: signal box, footbridge, goods wagon
in the siding, the roof of station house visible behind hedges.
I'm walking down the lane that never had a name where a huge
ash dwarfs the entrance to the back yard. Flat roof extension,
the old timber shed built from creosote-leaking sleepers –
the garage we called it – a block outhouse with toilet attached,
open steel tank on top filled with rainwater, sludge, dead leaves,
and out in the field the black shed, caving in, where we fattened
pigs for market. A yard of gravel and muck with no path to the door.
Open it, what do you see? Bare rooms where all stories began.

Up the hall to the scullery and into the kitchen, flagged yellow
and red, blackened by years and the comings and goings of feet,
careless of time. Year after year we came and went as regular
as the trains, the house filling up only to empty again over time
like rainwater in a barrel. Now it is a shell, a perfect multiplicity
of difference, shaped around the body, snug and protective, warm
and affecting the senses in ways that can't be explained; the kitchen
hums an old song I can almost remember, cold as the pots that hang
in the scullery, warm as the coal-swallowing range. My voice strains
to meet it but can't reach the pitch of bubble and hiss, shallow
dripping of rainwater accumulating years of rust on the tongue.

I'm standing at the top of the road looking down on the car park,
the ghosts of fields, lanes and sheds, the invisible house, towering
over the rows of shining, insipid cars. All day they wait, suspended,
for something to happen, but nothing will. I walk around the lot –
I don't care who's watching – and try the back door. It opens,
as I knew it would, and I'm inside and everyone is here again.
There's no more waiting now; there will be time for all of us

to find the things we lost along the way, to learn the words of songs we longed to sing but never had the heart. And we will sound okay, better than we'd thought, and we will laugh at ourselves – and only at ourselves – and laughing share the joke with others.

Acknowledgements

Acknowledgement is due to the editors of the following publications in which a number of these poems, or versions of them, have appeared:

Poetry Ireland Review; Cyphers; Abridged; The Irish Times; Skylight 47; Crannóg Magazine; The Stony Thursday Book;14 Magazine; The Ofi Press; Shot Glass Journal; Boyne Berries; Drawn To The Light; Live Encounters; Honest Ulsterman; The Blue Nib; Bangor Literary Journal; Vox Galvia; The Cormorant; Poetry 24; Not The Time To Be Silent; Pendemic; Days of Clear Light (Salmon Poetry)*; 100 Words of Solitude* (Rare Swan Press)*; Empty House* (Doire Press).

"Belturbet Under Frost" was shortlisted in the formal category of the Poetry on the Lake Prize in 2021; "Hard Swallows" was highly commended in the Fingal Poetry Prize 2020; a film poem of "Staying Home," created by Pete McCluskey, was shortlisted for the Ó Bhéal Poetry Film Competition 2020; "Dog Days" was highly commended in the Westival Poetry Competition 2020; "Multiverse" was placed second in the Allingham Poetry Competition 2020; "The Invisible House" was runner up in the Trim Poetry Competition 2021.

"Fire & Flood" is my version of an immured sonnet, a form devised by the poet Philip Nikolayev.

My thanks to the Arts Council of Ireland for granting me an Agility Award in 2020 to write a sequence of formal poems on the Covid 19 pandemic, some of which are included in this collection. I'd like to also acknowledge the support of Listowel Writers' Week for providing a writing bursary to attend Cill Rialaig writers' retreat in February 2023 where an early draft of the title poem was written.

I also want to extend my sincere thanks to John Murphy who continues to be an enthusiastic first reader and generous mentor and advisor. Thanks also go to my fellow poets at the Hibernian Poetry Workshop whose advice and encouragement are always appreciated. I'm particularly grateful to Amanda Bell and Jane Robinson for engaging with the collection and agreeing to write some kind words for the cover. My thanks also to artist, Rosaleen Fleming, for permission to use the wonderful cover image. Once again, I want to express my gratitude to Jessie Lendennie and Siobhán Hutson at Salmon Poetry for the service they render to all supporters and lovers of poetry.

Lastly, I'd like to thank my incredible family for continuing to allow me the time and space to pursue my meanderings.

BRIAN KIRK is an award-winning poet, short story writer and novelist from Dublin. His first poetry collection *After The Fall* was published by Salmon Poetry in 2017. His poem "Birthday" won the Listowel Writers' Week Irish Poem of the Year at the Irish Book Awards 2018. His short fiction chapbook *It's Not Me, It's You* won the Southword Fiction Chapbook Competition and was published by Southword Editions in 2019. He is a recipient of Professional Development and Agility Awards from the Arts Council of Ireland. His novel *Riverrun* was chosen as a winner of the Irish Writers Centre Novel Fair 2022 and was shortlisted for the Spotlight First Novel Award 2023. His poetry has been published in the *Irish Times, Poetry Ireland Review, Cyphers, Abridged, Skylight 47, Crannóg* and many others. His poetry has been featured on The Poetry Programme on RTÉ Radio One, the Words Lightly Spoken Podcast and the Poetry Jukebox installations in Limerick and Derry in 2023 as part of the Poetry As Commemoration strand. Brian has been a guest author and hosted events at literary festivals around the country including Dublin Book Festival, Listowel Writers' Week, Red Line Book Festival, Cork Short Story Festival, Ó Bhéal Winter Warmer Poetry Festival, Belfast Book Festival and Bray Literary Festival. He is a member of the Hibernian Writers' Group. www.briankirkwriter.com.

Photo: Martha Kirk

salmonpoetry
Cliffs of Moher, County Clare, Ireland

"Publishing the finest Irish and international literature."
Michael D. Higgins, President of Ireland